OUR DANCE

JD, TH – For Ella and Arlo

A Lothian Children's Book
Published in Australia and New Zealand in 2025
by Hachette Australia
Gadigal Country, Level 17, 207 Kent Street, Sydney, NSW 2000
www.hachettechildrens.com.au

Hachette Australia acknowledges and pays our respects to the past, present and future Traditional Owners and Custodians of Country throughout Australia and recognises the continuation of cultural, spiritual and educational practices of Aboriginal and Torres Strait Islander peoples. Our head office is located on the lands of the Gadigal people of the Eora Nation.

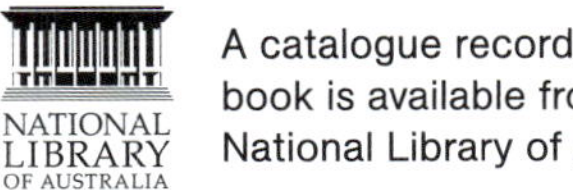

A catalogue record for this book is available from the National Library of Australia

ISBN: 978 0 7344 2342 9 (hardback)

Designed by Jo Hunt
Colour reproduction by Splitting Image
Printed in China by Toppan Leefung Printing

JACINTA DANIHER · TAYLOR HAMPTON

OUR DANCE

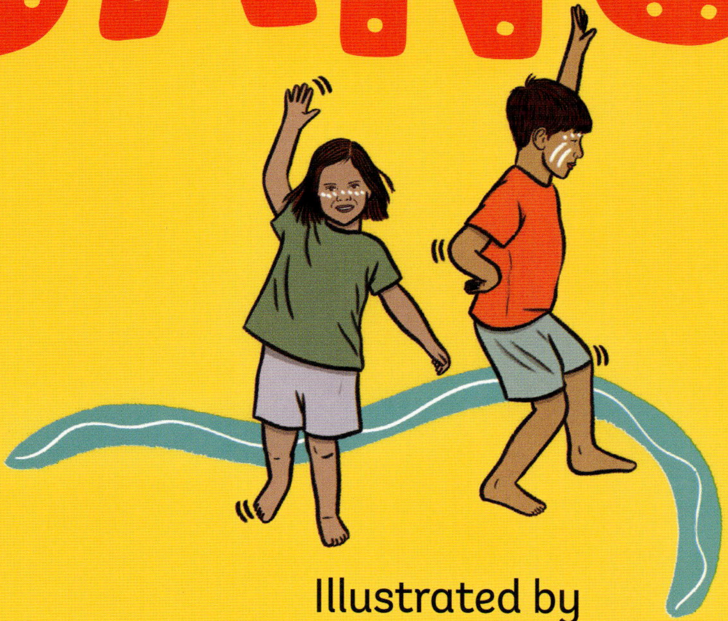

Illustrated by
JANELLE BURGER

Under the moon, by the big gum tree,
Let's **dance** and sing in the corroboree.

With ochre on our bodies, Our **dance** awaits,

Our mob, Our culture, let's celebrate.

Shake a leg, feel the **beat**,
Celebrate the land beneath our feet.
Listen to the Yidaki play,
A rhythmic tune that leads the way.

Our bodies move, proud and strong,
To the **rhythm** we all belong.

We move like animals, wild and free,
Telling stories of **The Dreaming**, come and see.

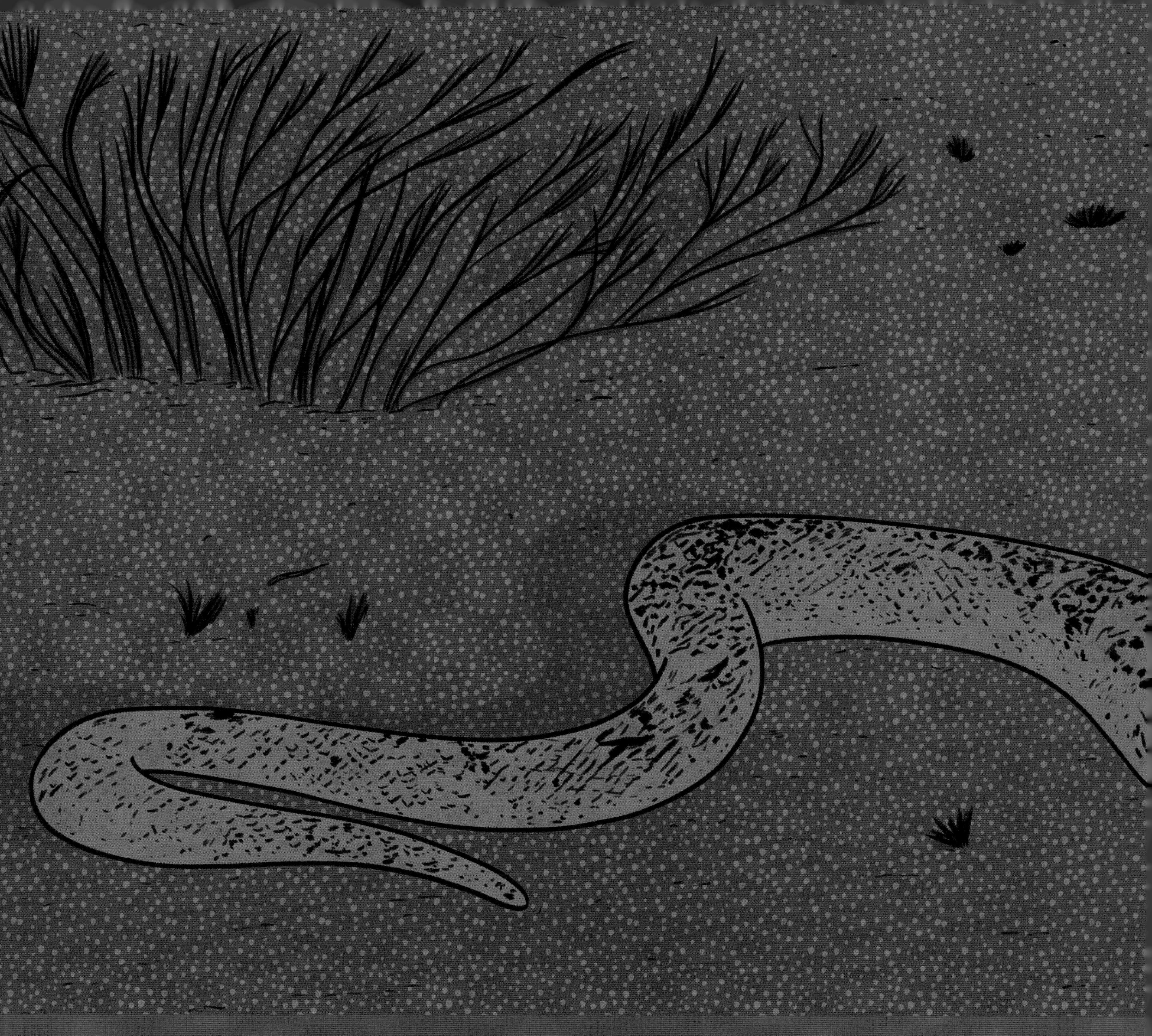

Slither like a snake under the sun,

Come join in, it will be so fun.

Stretch your arms with such pride,

Slither and **slither**, side to side.

If you want to **dance** like a kangaroo,

Listen close, here's what you do.

Jump, jump, jump, don't miss a beat,

Bounce, bounce, bounce, feel the rhythm in your feet.

In the outback, underneath the sun,
A goanna **moves**, its day begun.

Let's **move** our body low to the ground,

Creeping and **crawling** without a sound.

An emu is so wild and free,
Running **fast**, as **fast** as can be.

Make a tail feather using your hand,

And **dance** like an emu upon this land.

Look, it's an eagle way up high,
Soaring freely through the sky.

Spread your arms out, wide as you can,

Flying and **gliding** over our ancient land.

Come on, you mob, let's join in,
Our **dance** is ready, let's begin.

Slither like a snake,
Jump like a roo,

Crawl like a goanna,
Run, **Run** emu too,

And **Fly**, eagle, **Fly**.

Our **dance**, Our **celebration**, has begun,
Thank you for joining us, we hope you've had fun!